Men-at-Arms • 218

PREY
SHING

Ancient Chinese Armies 1500–200 BC

C J Peers • Illustrated by Angus McBride

Series editor Martin Windrow

First published in Great Britain in 1990 by
Osprey Publishing, Midland House,
West Way, Botley, Oxford OX2 0PH, UK
443 Park Avenue South, New York, NY 10016, USA
Email: info@ospreypublishing.com

Reprinted 1991, 1996, 1998, 2000, 2002, 2003, 2004, 2005

British Library Cataloguing in Publication Data
Peers, C. J.
Ancient Chinese Armies, 1500–200 BC.
1. China. Military equipment
I. Title II. Series
623'.0931
ISBN 0-85045-942-7

Series Editor: MARTIN WINDROW

Filmset in Great Britain
Printed in China through World Print Ltd.

FOR A CATALOGUE OF ALL BOOKS PUBLISHED BY OSPREY MILITARY AND AVIATION PLEASE CONTACT:

NORTH AMERICA
Osprey Direct, 2427 Bond Street,
University Park, IL 60466, USA
E-mail: info@ospreydirectusa.com

ALL OTHER REGIONS
Osprey Direct UK, P.O. Box 140,
Wellingborough, Northants, NN8 2FA, UK
E-mail: info@ospreydirect.co.uk

www.ospreypublishing.com

Artist's Note

Readers may care to note that the original paintings from which the colour plates in this book were prepared are available for private sale. All reproduction copyright whatsoever is retained by the Publishers. All enquiries should be addressed to:

Scorpio
PO Box 475,
Hailsham,
E. Sussex BN27 2SL

The Publishers regret that they can enter into no correspondence upon this matter.

Erratum: Plate E1 shows a transverse helmet crest; this should probably be mounted fore-and-aft.

Ancient Chinese Armies 1500-200 BC

Introduction

The subject of this book is the period of China's history from the first documented civilisation to the establishment of an enduring unified empire. For most of this period China—'All Under Heaven', as it was known—was no more than a vague cultural concept embracing a number of states linked only by a uniform system of writing, and differing markedly in politics, religion and language. It is often difficult to decide whether a particular state or people should be treated as 'Chinese' at all, and in this respect I have followed somewhat arbitrary traditional guidelines. Thus the Wu and Yueh of the south-east have been covered, but northern tribes like the Hu and Ti are mentioned only in passing, although they also fell within what is now China.

The study of the period is still at a formative stage, but much archaeological work has been done in China recently, and bronze weapons and figurines are well represented in museums, as well as in an increasing flow of illustrated books coming out of the People's Republic. A number of ancient written sources are available in translation, of which the most useful are cited in the Bibliography, although the problem of their reliability is a complex one. The *Shu Ching* ('Book of Documents'), *Shi Ching* ('Book of Songs') and *Chou Li* ('Rituals of Chou') all date from late in the period, but contain much early first-millennium material; while the 4th-century military manuals of Sun Tzu and Wu Ch'i are indispensable. The *Tso Chuan*, consisting of Tso Ch'u-ming's commentaries on the 'Spring and Autumn Annals' of the state of Lu, and *Chan-Kuo Ts'e*, the 'Intrigues of the Warring States', are semi-fictional but almost contemporary accounts, and the former in particular contains much useful and convincing military information. The general integrity of written sources is illustrated by the remarkable correspondence between the list of Shang kings given by the Han historian Ssu-ma Ch'ien, a millennium after their deaths, and the names found on oracle-bones excavated from Shang sites. These bones and pieces of tortoiseshell, on which inscriptions were made for divinatory purposes, are a vital archaeological source for the Shang.

I have also consulted many modern works, although space prevents me citing more than a few. I must emphasise, however, that my opinions on some questions, such as the importance of infantry in early times, do not always correspond with those generally accepted. It is for the reader who wishes to study the subject in more detail to reach his or her own conclusions, but I hope that I have at least pointed out some directions for future research and debate.

I have adopted the popular Wade-Giles system for transcribing Chinese names into English, but there is no universally accepted system, and readers should beware of being misled by different versions of these names in other works. For example, the state which I have called Tsin will appear elsewhere as Jin or Chin (not to be confused with Ch'in), while Shou, the last Shang

These figures from oracle-bone inscriptions are an important source for the appearance of Shang military equipment, especially perishable items such as shields—see reconstructions in Plate A. (Thames and Hudson Ltd.)

king and enemy of the Chou dynasty, is often confusingly called Chou. There is little point in giving any guide to pronunciation, since ancient Chinese was pronounced quite differently from the modern language and would have borne little relation to the way in which it is now transcribed.

Chronology

c.1500 BC Introduction of advanced bronze-casting. Rise of Shang state.
c.1300 BC Introduction of chariot. Permanent Shang capital established at Yin.
c.1027 BC Chou revolt. Battle of Mu. Chou conquest of central China.
c.880 BC Hsung K'eu of Ch'u takes title of 'king'. Chou king forces him to give it up and reduces him to vassalage.
771 BC Invasion by Jung barbarians. Fall of Chou capital, Hao. Eastern Chou dynasty established at Lo-yi; kingdom divided into two parts.
750 BC Chou kingdom reunited by King P'ing.
707 BC King Huan defeated by rebel ministers at Hsu-ko. Chou realm fragments into hundreds of small states.
685–643 BC Duke Huan of Ch'i, first hegemon.
632 BC Tsin defeats Ch'u at Ch'eng-p'u.
595 BC Ch'u defeats Tsin at Pi.
584 BC Wu-ch'en of Ch'u organises Wu army on Chinese lines.
576 BC Ch'in expedition decisively defeated by Tsin at Ma-sui.
575 BC Tsin defeats Ch'u at Yen-ling.
506 BC Wu invades Ch'u. Fall of Ying.
479 BC Death of Confucius.
473 BC Yueh overruns and destroys Wu.
453 BC Coalition of ex-allies defeats Tsin at Ching Yang. Tsin breaks up into three parts—Wei, Han and Chao.
350 BC Lord Shang begins his political and military reforms in Ch'in.
333 BC Ch'u conquers Yueh.
318 BC Coalition led by Ch'u crushed by Ch'in.
316 BC Ch'in conquers Shu and Pa.
307 BC Wu Ling of Chao forms China's first cavalry units.
285 BC Yen overruns Ch'i.
279 BC Yen defeated at Chi Mo and expelled from Ch'i.
256 BC Ch'in deposes the Chou king. Official end of Chou dynasty.
246 BC Accession of King Cheng in Ch'in.
223 BC Final defeat of Ch'u by Ch'in.
221 BC Ch'in conquers Ch'i. China unified under King Cheng, the First Emperor.
210 BC Death of the First Emperor.
207 BC Ch'u rebels destroy Ch'in army at Hsin-an. Second Emperor commits suicide.
206 BC Ch'in dynasty disintegrates. China divided between Hsiang Yu and Liu Pang.
202 BC Liu Pang defeats Hsiang Yu and proclaims Han dynasty. China reunited.

Note: All dates before 841 BC are approximate. I have here adopted the chronology based on the 'Bamboo Annals' of the 3rd century BC, which is favoured by more modern scholars, as well as being easier to reconcile with external influences, than the dates derived from Ssu-ma Ch'ien, who would place e.g. the battle of Mu in 1122 BC.

The Shang Dynasty

Although later tradition describes a revolt of the Shang people against an even earlier dynasty, the Hsia, culminating in the Battle of Ming T'iao in 1763 BC, it is only with the introduction of writing under the Shang that China emerges from prehistory. By the 15th century BC the valley of the Hwang Ho was dominated by a palace-based military caste which owed its supremacy to a monopoly of bronze-working techniques among a still mainly Stone Age population. There is no direct evidence for the origin of this new technology, but similarities in weapon-types suggest that it diffused into northern China via

Siberia and Manchuria. The Shang themselves, however, were certainly indigenous, as their styles of art and writing show. Their original centre of power may have been in modern Shantung, but they moved their early wooden palaces frequently, perhaps to avoid the notorious Hwang Ho floods, gradually drifting north and east down the valley. As they did so they brought an increasing number of neighbouring tribes under their rule. Shang culture as well as political influence spread over a wide area of north China, but did not yet constitute a centralised state.

The 'Book of Documents' describes a Shang sphere of influence stretching from the sea in the east to the sand deserts of the west, but only the area within a hundred miles or so of the capital was under direct royal control. Outside this were provinces ruled by Shang-influenced local nobles who often fought with each other or even with the king himself. Still further out were 'allied barbarians', mostly semi-nomadic Yi tribes which had not yet adopted Shang culture but were at least temporarily overawed; and, beyond them, the 'wild' nomads. It is likely, however, that the distinction between 'Chinese' and 'barbarians' was less clear than it later became, and that the Shang themselves were a pastoral people, relying as much on their herds of sheep, cattle and horses as on their crops.

War was a means of legitimising the power of the new aristocracy, and the main aim of foreign policy was the sending out of expeditions to parade this power and gather tribute. Surrounding peoples were deliberately left unconquered to serve as an excuse for war and a reservoir of booty and prisoners; the maintenance of a steady supply of captives was important to the Shang state, as its religion relied heavily on human sacrifice. This represents a primitive stage in the evolution of international relations, in which the resources of other communities at a lower technological level are exploited in a manner analogous to a hunting expedition. In fact hunting trips and military campaigns were organised in the same way, and the distinction between them was often blurred.

The Shang nobility was held together by a complicated clan system, royal power apparently alternating among the members of ten of these clans. This arrangement sometimes led to civil strife, but the period as a whole was one of gradual increase in state power. In about 1300 BC King Pan-k'eng moved the capital to Yin, where it was to remain until the fall of the dynasty. The palace-cities were by now on a considerable scale; it has been estimated that the defences of the 15th-century city of Ao would have taken 10,000 men 18 years to build.

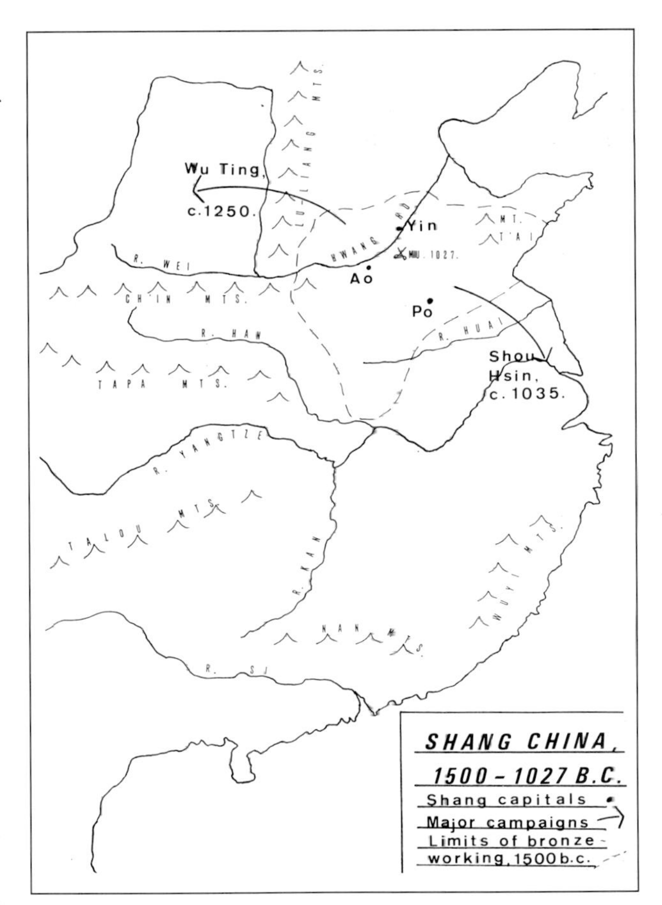

By the 13th century, Shang influence had spread upriver to what is now Kansu Province, a region occupied by the people known as the Chou. The Chou adopted a compromise between the culture of the Shang and that of the steppe further west. They used bronze, and may have had chariots before the Shang. Certainly their vehicles were better made, and they had more horses. At first they appear as Shang vassals, but by the 11th century their strength had greatly increased. In about 1040 BC their ruler, Wen, was given the title 'Count of the West' by the Shang king Shou Hsin, who trusted Wen to guard his rear while he was involved in a campaign in the

Bone arrowhead from the early Shang dynasty, about $3\frac{3}{4}$ in. long (9.5cm). (Reproduced by courtesy of the Trustees of the British Museum, as are all illustrations in this book credited to the Museum.)

south-east. Shou is described in Chou records as a depraved tyrant, but he may have been right to fear the growing power of Wen, who by now controlled two-thirds of the realm. At any rate, Shou imprisoned him, and Wen's son Wu led the Chou in revolt. The decisive battle was fought in 1027 BC in the wilderness of Mu. Wu occupied the central Hwang Ho valley, building forts at Hao and Lo to hold his conquests, and proclaimed the Chou dynasty. Later Chou propaganda depicts the Shang people as welcoming him as a liberator, but other data cast doubt on this. Shou had been killed, but his son led a revolt which took three years to suppress, and fighting continued in the east for generations. Eventually a Shang successor state, Sung, was allowed to survive on the lower Hwang Ho, although it soon adopted Chou military methods.

The Shang army

Shang expeditions mentioned on the oracle-bones averaged 3,000 to 5,000 strong, but in emergencies forces of up to 30,000 could be raised. Evidence for the appearance of Shang warriors can be gleaned from the pictographs used in inscriptions, as well as from a few surviving statuettes and excavated items of armour. Weapons included bows, spears, and the *ko* or dagger-axe—a primitive weapon consisting of a blade mounted at right angles to a three- to six-foot shaft and usually used one-handed together with a shield. Conventional axes were known, but were less popular. Spears were around seven feet long, and had bronze blades; the jade spearheads often found are too brittle for combat, and presumably had a ceremonial function.

The composite recurved bow was known, usually made of strips of bamboo glued or bound together with silk and averaging four feet long. Arrows were of reed or bamboo, tipped with bronze or bone; the metal did not completely replace bone for this purpose until very late in the Shang period. Knives and daggers, often very ornate, are common in aristocratic graves. These also were originally made from bone, often that of human sacrifices, but by the 13th century bronze was more usual. Nobles could wear armour; in the early Shang this mainly consisted of breastplates made from pieces of shell tied together, but again bronze became popular later on. Bronze helmets, usually decorated with monstrous faces cast in

Bronze knife, about 24.5cm long, probably used by a Shang charioteer. The design of the handle suggests Central Asian influence. (British Museum)

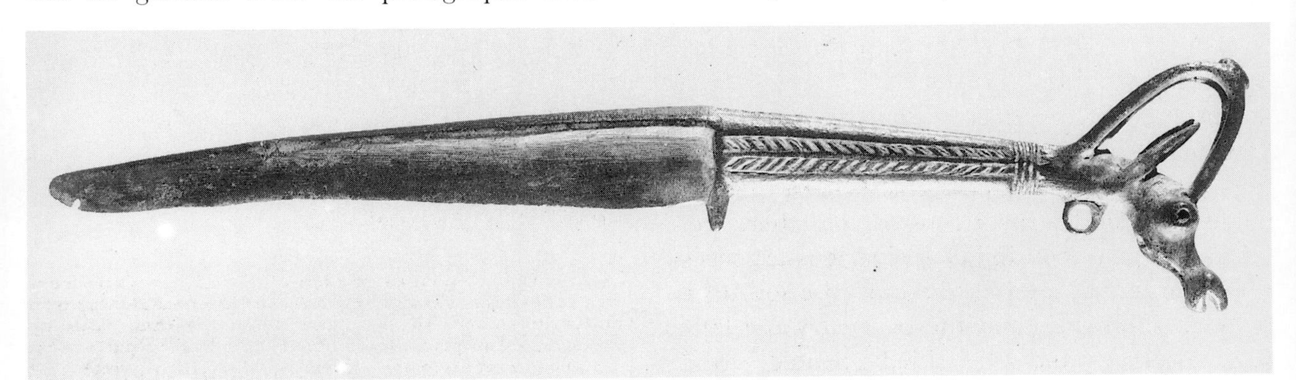

relief, were rarer, and the rank and file probably did without any protection except for a leather shield stretched over a bamboo frame.

The chariot, probably an import from Central Asia, first appeared at around the time of the foundation of Yin, but was always restricted to the aristocracy. A 12th-century inscription listing the spoils of a campaign in the west gives an idea of the likely proportions: 1,570 prisoners, 15 pieces of armour, but only two chariots. Shang vehicles were drawn by two horses, although four are occasionally found in burials. The crew consisted of an archer, a driver, and often a third man armed with a spear or dagger-axe. Only the harness decorations, part of the yoke and the axle-caps of the chariots were bronze, the rest being wood, lashed or pegged together. Wheels were up to five feet in diameter with 18 or more spokes; the cab of the vehicle was low and open-fronted, enclosed only by rails. Horses were small and large-headed, reminiscent of the wild Przewalski breed of Mongolia, and were controlled by a bit and bridle made of rope.

A final possible constituent of Shang armies was the war elephant. Elephants of the Indian variety were wild in central China until the first millennium BC, and were certainly captured alive on occasions. A very old tradition ascribes the use of elephants to a minister of the legendary King Yao on a campaign against the southern tribes; and a later legend has the minister, Shun, conquering a wild brother known as Hsiang ('Elephant') by kindness. It is likely that these stories were based on a genuine memory of the use of the beasts in war, in which case it must have originated with the Shang, the first dynasty to fight in the central and southern regions where they were found. The tactic probably did not catch on because of the rapid decline due to hunting of the wild elephant, which is difficult to breed in captivity, and its limited usefulness against foes well equipped with missiles.

Armies were recruited and equipped on an organised basis. Weapon and chariot manufacture was under royal control, and there were officials with responsibility for various aspects of raising an army. Despite the immense social gap between the nobles and the peasantry the latter were not slaves, and were called up to fight when

Bronze weapons, such as this Shang dagger-axe blade from north-east China, survive much better than their later iron counterparts, and so their original appearance can be reconstructed in great detail. Note the intricate pattern on the blade. About 24cm overall length. (British Museum)

Shang, battle accounts emphasising chariot archery; but the Chou had their own distinctive styles of armour. These are described in the 'Rituals of Chou', which lays down guidelines for the palace armourers. One type, the *kia*, was a sleeveless coat of rhinoceros or buffalo hide formed on a wooden dummy, while another kind was known as *kiai* and consisted of leather scales on a fabric backing. This was used for corselets and armoured trappers for chariot horses, which were also protected by tiger skins. Chou bronze helmets were similar to Shang types but less elaborately decorated, and it is thought that the hood-shaped styles of the later Han dynasty were metal copies of older leather versions.

Bronze frontlet, approx. 29cm long, part of a set of armour for a chariot horse, Western Chou dynasty. An alternative design is shown in Plate B. (British Museum)

The army consisted of contingents supplied according to strict rules by vassal states. Vassals of the first rank had to provide three armies, those of the second, two, and third-rank states, one. The size of these forces is not known, but a large army of the Western Chou could field up to 3,000 chariots and 30,000 infantry. The chariot-riding nobility were the mainstay of the army, but the common people also had a vital rôle. The 'Book of Changes', a work of divination dating from the early Chou, uses as a metaphor for the army the image of water hidden under the earth, referring to the military power represented by the peasantry, and emphasises the need to deal fairly with the people in order to retain their loyalty. This conflicts with the traditional view that Chou warfare was essentially an aristocratic game, and implies that the later development of mass armies was a logical continuation of the Chou system.

Further evidence comes from the 'Book of Songs', where the peasants are described as undergoing a month's military training every year; and from the account in the 'Book of Documents' of the Chou army at the Battle of Mu, where Wu ordered his men to advance slowly in ranks and halt at intervals to keep their order. These do not sound like chariot tactics, and the passage may point to a much more highly developed rôle for infantry than is generally assumed. Confucian tradition relates that the Chou organised farmers in their domains into a system known as *ching-t'ien* or 'well-field', according to which each unit of eight families grouped round a well had to provide one recruit for the army. The system must have existed, but the version which we have is an idealisation which was probably never rigidly adhered to.

The Shang system of small-unit organisation was apparently retained. At Hsu-ko chariots were deployed in units of 25, each vehicle protected by 25 infantrymen in five ranks. Armies were generally divided into three divisions, left, right and centre, perhaps corresponding to the 'armies' which vassals were required to provide. In later periods the left took precedence, but early Chou generals were usually found in the centre.

The Eastern Chou

The period between 770 and 256 BC is known as the Eastern Chou after the capital at Lo-yi. It is traditionally divided into two sub-periods: the 'Springs and Autumns', after the annals of the state of Lu, up to 479, and the 'Warring States' thereafter. A distinction is often drawn between the chivalrous, aristocratic warfare of the former period and the mass armies and ruthless professionalism of the latter. In fact the true picture was one of steady evolution, and plenty of examples can be found of ruthless generalship as early as the 8th century, and of individual heroics as late as the 3rd. Certainly there was never much respect for the rights of the smaller states, which began to be swallowed up by stronger neighbours from the 720s onwards, and where permitted to survive were usually impressed into one of the alliances led by the major powers. The hundreds of independent states were reduced by the fifth century to only eight of any consequence: Ch'in, Ch'i, Ch'u, Yueh, Yen, Han, Wei and Chao, the last three having been formed from the breakup of the old great power of the Hwang Ho valley, Tsin. There were many reasons for the success of these states, but it is significant that all were originally on the periphery of the Chinese world, and were able to expand outwards and increase their strength by assimilating barbarian peoples. The ruling house of Tsin, for example, was originally a clan of the Ti tribe, while Ch'i built up its power in the 6th century by incorporating the Yi of the Shantung Peninsula. Ch'in, Ch'u and Yueh in particular were so under barbarian influence that it was a long time before their neighbours recognised them as Chinese at all; but from the time of their first appearance in history they had adopted local forms of the political and military institutions of the central states.

The Chinese/barbarian distinction was still very unclear, and tribes usually regarded as barbarian existed between and within organised states, living in towns and maintaining chariot forces like the true Chinese, and often supplying them with allies. The Ti, for example, fought with Ch'i against Wei in 640, and with Tsin against Ch'in in 601. After the 6th century, however, most of these tribes were absorbed or banished to the arid borderlands, and the survivors appear in Chinese records mainly as enemies.

The 8th to the 5th centuries were the time of greatest cultural differences between the states, but internally they were becoming more centralised as a civil service based on merit

Light axes were a popular sidearm in early China; this example, from its elaborate decoration probably belonging to a noble charioteer, dates from around 700 BC. (British Museum)

shoot again when Shing called to him, saying that it was unchivalrous to take two shots without allowing him to defend himself. P'ao lowered his bow, and was immediately shot dead.

Organisation and tactics were highly developed. The traditional three divisions were still used, but this could be varied if necessary. At Che in 717 three Cheng forces were used to pin the enemy frontally while a fourth worked its way round the flank; while in 540 Tsin fought in five bodies against the Ti. Infantry were deployed five deep, either with the chariots or as a body in the centre; and a remark in 'Wu Ch'i's Art of War', that tall men were given missile weapons and shorter men spears and halberds, implies that archers could be deployed behind the spearmen to shoot overhead. Tactical formations such as 'crane and goose' and 'fish-scale' are mentioned, the latter placing the chariots in line in front with infantry behind. All arms were subjected to a ferocious code of discipline; in 540, for instance, a Tsin nobleman was beheaded for refusing to fight on foot when ordered.

Continuous warfare accelerated developments in weapons and equipment. The chariot still carried three crewmen—a driver, an archer on the left, and a man armed with spear or dagger-axe on the right. Wheels now had up to 26 spokes, and the old nine-foot chariot pole, a source of structural weakness, was shortened to six feet. Cabs were covered with leather to protect the crew, and a canopy or parasol began to make its appearance, although this may have been removed in battle. Four horses were now standard. Some chariots were also equipped with serrated bronze blades about a foot long on the axle-caps. Paradoxically, despite the increase in vehicle numbers, archaeological finds of bronze chariot-fittings are much rarer from the Eastern Chou than from earlier centuries; this may reflect the fact that chariots were now state property and were reused rather than buried with their owners, but it is also likely that they had become more functional and less hampered with excessive decoration.

Armour and bows were similar to earlier types, but the dagger-axe continued to evolve, and by the 4th century the addition of a spear-blade to the end of the shaft had turned it into a true cut-and-thrust weapon or halberd. Spears and dagger-axes fell into two groups, one about nine feet long, the other around 18 feet. Swords were still of the short stabbing type; blades were still bronze, but from the 5th century iron began to appear, the states of Ch'u and Han being known for their weapons of low-grade steel. Iron smelting technology, however, remained very primitive until the 2nd century BC, and the metal could not replace bronze for most military purposes.

Another development of this period was the crossbow, ascribed to Ch'in Shih of Ch'u in the 6th century. The maximum range of this weapon was said to be 600 paces, but its advantage over

Blade for chariot axle, 5th to 4th centuries. Although the Chinese chariot was not designed for breaking up infantry formations in the manner of the scythed Persian variety, such an attachment would deter infantrymen trying to climb aboard, and might damage the wheels of enemy chariots not so equipped. (British Museum)

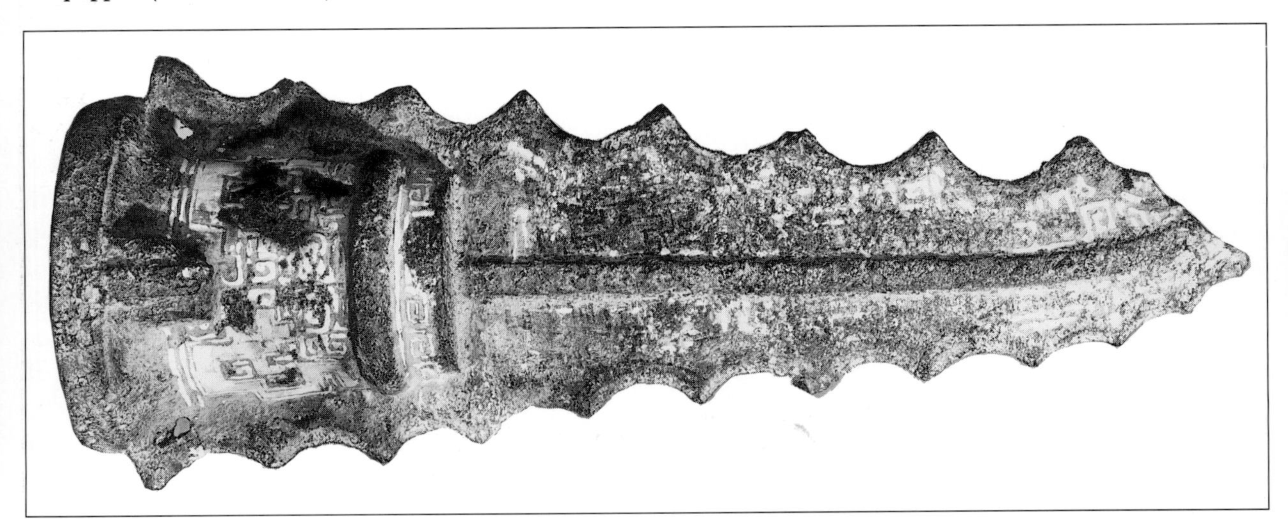

the conventional bow lay in its penetrating power at short range, and because of its slow rate of fire it was at first most popular for defending towns. By 340, however, it was in use in pitched battles and may have contributed to the decline of the chariot, which as a large, slow-moving target, protected only by leather, must have been very vulnerable.

Two peculiarities of southern warfare in this period are of interest: the use of convicts and of elephants. Wu pioneered the employment of condemned criminals as suicide troops at Ke-fu in 518, when 300 were lined up in the van and launched in an attack on the Ch'u army before it was properly deployed. At Tsui-le in 496 the Yueh went one better when, unable to break the Wu line, they sent three ranks of convicts out between the armies. These unfortunates were threatened with reprisals against their families, given swords, and ordered to cut their own throats. The Wu troops, transfixed by this gruesome sight, were taken unawares and overrun by the Yueh. Southern warfare in general was waged with a savagery unknown to the

Relief on 5th-century vessel, showing scenes of archery practice (top left), siege warfare (bottom right), and an amphibious battle (bottom left). Wu and Yueh in particular were great naval powers, and often accompanied their invasions of Ch'u with large river-based fleets. Note the standards (lower left) resembling leafy branches attached to spears or staffs. These are common in early art, also being shown flown from the rear of chariots, and are presumably the yak-tail standards mentioned in written sources. (Thames and Hudson Ltd.)

B

Chariot, Western Chou, c.800 BC

Eastern Chou warriors, 700 BC-400 BC:
1: Lord's bodyguard
2: Infantry archer

1

2

Western warriors, 300 BC-200 BC:
1: Chao horseman
2: Tien warrior

F

The Ch'in Imperial Guard, 221 BC-206 BC:
1: Crossbowman
2: Halberdier
3: Skirmisher

G

Tactical & Strategic Doctrine

A number of ancient Chinese works on military science survive. The best known are those attributed to Sun Tzu, whose author supposedly lived about 500 BC but which may be 4th century; and Wu Ch'i, traditionally a work of the 380s but in fact a compilation containing much 3rd-century material. However, 182 such books were known in the early Han period, and 'Tso Chuan' describes Sun Shuh of Ch'u as quoting a manual called 'The Art of War' as early as the Battle of Pi in 595. Written works containing a formal system of strategy and tactics were therefore not, as is sometimes assumed, an invention of the 'Warring States' era.

The *Sun Tzu Ping Fa*, or 'Sun Tzu's Art of War', was by far the most influential of these books, and can be considered to contain the essence of Chinese thinking on the subject. It was not, however, without its critics. The philosopher Han Fei Tzu, whose ideas influenced King Cheng of Ch'in, felt that it placed too little emphasis on the rôle of discipline in controlling troops, and that its humane concern with the limitation of war was hypocritical. The Confucians, on the other hand, were horrified by its advocacy of deceit and covert operations. Yet to a modern reader it is remarkable for its rational approach and lucid exposition of the critical factors in warfare.

According to the 'Sun Tzu', the first requirement for a campaign is a mathematical calculation of the respective strengths of the combatants, with weighting where appropriate for factors such as the ability of commanders and the social cohesion of states. If it was decided to embark on war, it was essential to carry the fighting into enemy territory. This had three advantages: it enabled troops to live off the land without antagonising one's own people, it disrupted the enemy's mobilisation plans, and it reduced desertion by one's own men, whose best hope of safety in a hostile country was to stay with the army. This implies that commanders were often unsure of the reliability of their troops; and Sun Tzu frequently returns to this subject, suggesting that the army be deliberately led into 'death ground', a desperate position where retreat is impossible, in order to induce it to fight.

Sun Tzu goes on to describe the terrible effects of a long war and to emphasise the need for speed in strategic operations. Pitched battles were to be avoided when possible and fortified cities to be bypassed, it being preferable to subvert an enemy by deceit, including the use of spies and secret agents. This type of operation was made easier by the fact that an inhabitant of one Chinese state could usually pass himself off as belonging to another. Knowledge of the enemy commander's character was vital for this sort of trickery, so that his personal weaknesses and vices could be used against him.

If battle is inevitable, Sun Tzu again stresses the importance of knowing the enemy, of reconnaissance, and of familiarity with the correct use of terrain. The 'Kuan Tzu', a 4th-century work, is even more emphatic on this latter point, and on the necessity for the detailed study of maps. The Shang may have had maps cast on bronze vessels, and by the Eastern Chou they were in widespread use, painted on silk. A magnetic compass, consisting of a piece of lodestone swinging freely on a wooden board, was also available by the 5th century at the latest.

Battle tactics revolved around the use of the 'ordinary' and 'extraordinary' forces. The main themes throughout the period are operations against the flanks and rear, and direct frontal attacks by deliberately enraged troops. All the surviving manuals discuss ways of assessing the state of the enemy from the appearance of his formations and the noise his men are making, and explain the need to judge the correct moment for a charge. Whatever the exact plan used, all sources stress the primacy of the offensive in ancient Chinese warfare, although field fortifications were often used as a base from which an attack could be launched, and many commanders entrenched their camps at night when in hostile territory. Sun Tzu therefore devotes a chapter to the use of fire as a method of

Figure of a crossbowman from the terracotta army of the First Emperor of Ch'in, as restored by Chinese archaeologists. A unique source for the military historian, the discovery of this buried army in 1974 revolutionised our understanding of the Ch'in army. See Plate G for a reconstruction based on this figure. (Cultural Relics Publishing House, Beijing)

Detail of surviving section of the 'Long Wall' of Wei, built in the 4th century, when Wei bore the brunt of Ch'in aggression. Note the stratified appearance created by the ramming down of successive layers of earth, a building technique used since Shang times. (Cultural Relics Publishing House, Beijing)

the *ch'ao-ch'e* or crow's-nest chariot, which was invented during the Eastern Chou. This consisted of a chariot with a high chassis and reinforced wheels, with a small tower on top. 'Tso Chuan' describes the king of Ch'u climbing on such a vehicle to observe the Tsin deployment in 575. It seems that the tower held only one man, as the king had to shout his observations to an officer below for interpretation.

Chinese troops were strictly controlled and drilled from an early date. The good order of the Chou army at Mu has already been mentioned, and the account in 'Tso Chuan' of the Ch'u army of 595 also bears witness to a developed system of drill. The troops could all manoeuvre at once in response to signals, and were trained to deploy in emergencies without specific orders. The introduction of marching in step has been associated with Wu Ch'i around 380, but may have taken place much earlier. A music manual of the 1st century BC describes a military dance of 'ancient times' in which the dancers advanced 'keeping together with perfect precision, like a military unit', the pace being regulated by the beat of a drum. Such dances were used as early as the Western Chou as training for war.

Fortification and sieges

The walled cities of the Shang represent the earliest Chinese fortifications. The walls were built by pounding earth with wooden rammers until it became as hard as brick; at Ao, they were 60 feet thick at the base and 25 feet in height. This technique was used until Ch'in times, but refinements were added later. By the 6th century lookout towers were being built above the walls, which could be faced with stone or brick. The area enclosed by the walls was traditionally square or rectangular, with a gate in the middle of each side; but the growth of towns in the Eastern Chou period led to the building of suburbs outside the walls, and these on occasion became the scene of furious battles. In some cases a series of concentric walls was erected at different times to enclose these suburbs.

The 'Book of Songs' describes methods used for assaulting towns in the Western Chou. Scaling ladders were available, including types which could be wheeled up to the walls, and protective mantlets were used to shield men attempting to tunnel through them. Starvation and assault by escalade remained the most popular ways of taking cities, although Kaou-yu in Lu was captured in 546 by Tsin troops creeping in through the storm-drains. By the 4th century, however, assaults were regarded as a last resort.

The defence had by then been strengthened by the invention of large artillery crossbows which were stationed on the walls. Some of these were cocked with pulleys and windlasses and had draw-weights of 400 pounds. In about 350 the 'Book of Lord Shang' described how the population of a beleaguered city was divided into three 'armies'; the able-bodied men guarded the ramparts, the women dug ditches and built earthworks, while the very young, old and infirm looked after the livestock. During the 4th century a new element was introduced into the defence by Mo Tzu, a philosopher who preached justice for the weak and was prepared to put his ideals into action. His works covered the techniques of defence and his followers, known as Mohists, intervened on numerous occasions on the side of small states which were under threat. Among their inventions were kites for signalling, improved pulleys and counterweight mechanisms, and a type of

A ruined tower on the Wei wall. (Cultural Relics Publishing House, Beijing)

primitive resonance box made from a pottery jar with a leather membrane over the mouth. These were buried in deep shafts within the walls, and by listening to the vibrations which they amplified it was possible to discover the direction and distance of enemy mining operations. Besiegers' tunnels, when located, were dealt with by burning noxious substances such as dried mustard in a furnace and blowing the smoke down the tunnels with oxhide bellows. Mo Tzu was able to prevent at least one war by demonstrating to the aggressor some of the techniques which he was prepared to use in support of the victim.

Another aspect of Chinese fortification was the building of long walls to protect a state's territory from attack. According to the 'Book of Songs' the Chou built a wall against the northern barbarians in the 8th century, and by the 5th the practice was widespread, as a protection not only against barbarians but against Chinese neighbours. Han, Wei, Chao, Ch'i, Yen, Ch'in, Chong-shan and Ch'u all had walls in the 4th century, some of which still survive in part despite the Ch'in Empire's demolition of internal barriers. Wei was defended against Ch'in by two parallel walls 180 yards apart, the outer being more than 20 feet thick. Square watchtowers were erected a bowshot beyond the outer wall. The walls and towers are now about 12 and 30 feet high respectively, but would originally have been considerably higher. The walls were made of rammed earth, the towers being strengthened with timber, and incorporating signal beacons to give warning of attack. All these constructions were crude compared to later versions, and few were continuous along the whole length of the borders; but the Ch'in wall started in 215 was a much more formidable obstacle, and at least in part seems to have taken the battlemented form familiar to us today, with room for vehicles to drive along the top. Even this barrier was probably guarded along most stretches only by outposts and patrols, however.

Although rebuilt many times, this north-eastern section of the Great Wall probably retains the main architectural features of the best parts of the Ch'in original. (Su Evans & Richard Patching)

Ten Decisive Battles

The following battles have been chosen to illustrate the Chinese art of war, both for their historical significance and for the light they shed on the tactics in use.

Mu, 1027 BC

Wu of Chou, leading an army of 3,000 nobles and their retainers, augmented by barbarian allies and 800 Shang defectors, met the Shang king Shou Hsin at Mu. The Shang force was considerably larger than that of the Chou. Wu therefore instructed his men to advance slowly and in strict formation; 'do not exceed four or five strokes, six or seven thrusts, then halt and line up'. The next morning the Shang attacked, but their front rank was thrown into confusion and fell back, disordering those behind. Despite the claims of Chou propaganda the battle was hard-fought, but the Chou were victorious and showed no mercy, shedding enough blood 'to float a log'. This battle made Wu master of most of the Hwang Ho valley.

Che, 717 BC

The southern Yen invaded Cheng in support of one of their allies, bypassing the town of Che. Three Cheng divisions were sent to occupy the enemy by skirmishing as they advanced, while a fourth body, under the earl's sons Man-pi and Tse-yuen, manoeuvred itself into their rear. The two princes entered Che undetected, and led the citizens in an attack which took the Yen by surprise and defeated them.

Cheng, 713 BC

The northern Jung, a foot-fighting barbarian tribe who were 'light and nimble, but had no order', invaded Cheng and were confronted by the earl. The Cheng charioteers feared that a swift attack would overrun them, so the earl's son Tu proposed a plan. The main body of the army was divided into three and withdrawn into positions for an ambush, and a detachment was sent forward to make a feint attack. This group pretended to flee and the Jung pursued in a disorderly mob. General Chu Tan ambushed the first body of barbarians to come within reach, and surrounded them. Tu had correctly judged the character of the enemy, for the rest of the Jung fled, making no attempt to help their comrades.

Ch'eng-p'u, 632 BC

Duke Wen of Tsin faced an invading army under Tzu-yu of Ch'u. The two men were personal enemies, and Tzu-yu led the chariots of his left wing with the aim of killing Wen. The Tsin left pinned the Ch'u right with a feint attack while their own right withdrew behind a screen of chariots dragging branches to raise dust. When Tzu-yu was well separated from his centre, the Tsin right and centre closed in on him from two sides with chariots and infantry. The Ch'u commander was killed and his army routed.

Pi, 595 BC

The Ch'u and Tsin armies faced each other for several days while the charioteers skirmished; the battle developed by accident when a force of Tsin chariots came out to rescue two of their skirmishers and the Ch'u charged them. Ch'u chariots advanced on both flanks, driving back their opponents when their reserve of 40 vehicles was committed, and the Tsin army began a general retirement. By chance, the king of Ch'u was with his left wing when it began to pursue, and from this time the left took precedence in Ch'u, a practice later followed by other states.

Operations against the enemy's rear: the Battle of Che, 717 BC.

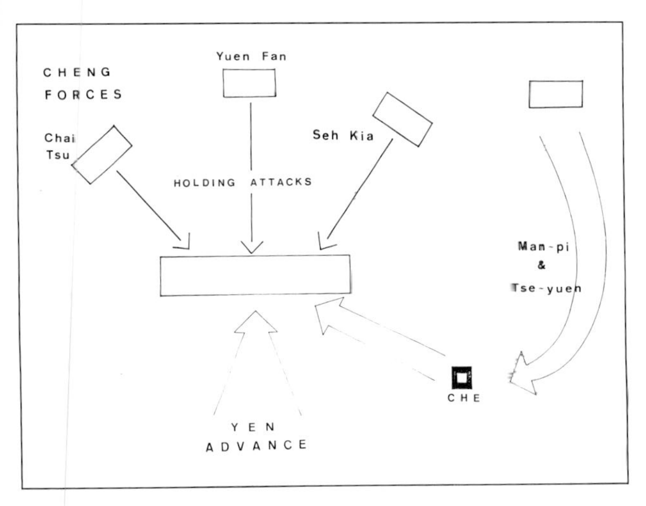

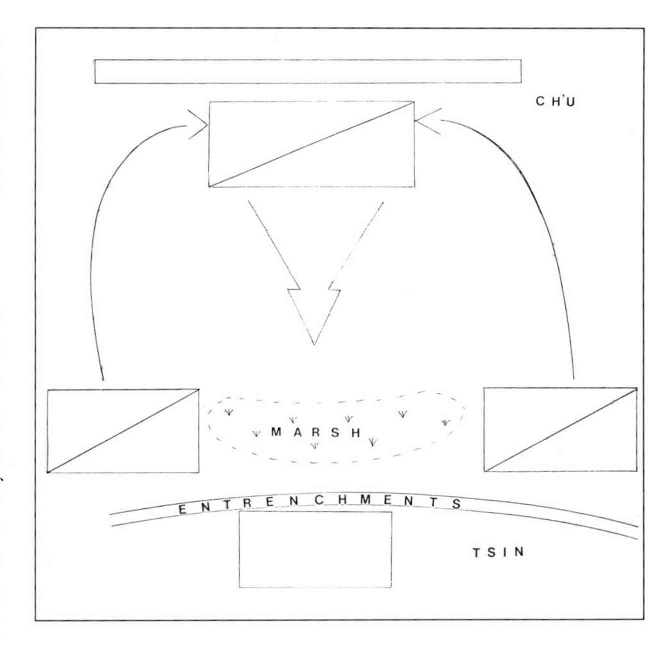

The battle of envelopment: Yen-ling, 575 BC.

Yen-ling, 575 BC

Ch'u once more confronted Tsin at Yen-ling, but the condition of the Ch'u army was poor. It contained many 'wild tribes of the south' who were badly disciplined, and the two ministers commanding it hated each other. The Tsin officer Meao Fun-hwang pointed out that the best Ch'u troops, those of the royal clan, were in the centre, and suggested an enveloping attack on both flanks while the Tsin centre stood on the defensive, protected by a marsh. This plan was successful and the Ch'u army was defeated.

P'ing-yin, 554 BC

Tsin beat a superior Ch'i army by deception. Deploying in close terrain, the Tsin soldiers set up banners in marshes and defiles where there were no troops, to make their line look longer than it was, and sent out patrols of carts dragging branches, and chariots with one crewman in each, the others being dummies. The Marquis of Ch'i, observing from Mount Wu, was convinced that he was outnumbered and decided to withdraw. The retreat was detected by the Tsin commander because of the activities of crows in the deserted camp, and he ordered a pursuit. Ch'i attempted to hold the pass of P'ing-yin against him, but the rearguard was taken prisoner and the main body harried back to Ch'i.

INDEX

(References to illustrations are shown in bold. Plates are shown with caption locators in brackets.)